KLIMT

T&J

This edition published 2011

Published by
TAJ BOOKS INTERNATIONAL LLP
27 Ferndown Gardens
Cobham
Surrey
KT11 2BH
UK
www.tajbooks.com

All notations of errors or omissions (author inquiries, permissions) concerning the content of this book should be addressed to info@tajbooks.com.

ISBN: 978-1-84406-169-3

KLIMT

BY SANDRA FORTY

"Whoever wants to know something about me—as an artist, the only notable thing—ought to look carefully at my pictures and try and see in them what I am and what I want to do."
Gustav Klimt

Fin-de-siècle Vienna was the capital of the Austro-Hungarian Empire, one of the strongest powers in Europe. It was a wealthy, exciting city of changing politics and a vibrant culture. Fevered struggles took place between traditionalists and modernists each trying to propel their vision and attitudes into the new century. One of the greatest and most celebrated bringers of change was Gustav Klimt, an artist of rare innovation and technique whose work was criticised by many as being little short of pornographic. Although many of his paintings can be interpreted that way, such a simple dismissal of his compositions completely misses his genius and delicacy of technique.

Klimt started as a generic history artist painting popular cultural subjects with great skill and ability but little innovation. He established a good name for himself in Vienna painting murals and portraits, and in the process made himself a fairly wealthy man. Then something inside him changed and he started developing his own unique style that emphasized line and pattern and covered much more mystical, elusive subjects. Central to almost all his paintings were exotically beautiful women, wearing few if any clothes but rather sheathed behind layers of veils and diaphanous materials. The fact that many of these women were at least partially naked and sometimes wrapped in ambiguous embrace or deep in sated sleep, led to the accusations of pornography. Additionally, Klimt loaded rich layers of refined and elaborate ornament and pattern into his work that made allusions to deeper meanings. The results were elegant, deeply mysterious but sensuous paintings that some people found unsettling but many more considered the work of a genius.

Such paintings established Klimt as an important Symbolist and one of the leaders of the Austrian *Sezession* (Secession) movement. The Modernist Viennese artists grouped together as the Secession with Klimt very much as their inspiration and leading light. He brought international attention and recognition to Viennese Modernism and was its best-known spokesman.

The Secessionists were the Austrian equivalent of the Art Nouveau artists of France or the Jugendstil artists of Germany, but unlike them their worldview was more akin to the earlier British Arts and Crafts movement. They embraced all types of craftsmen under their umbrella not just painters and sculptors, but also graphic designers and illustrators, architects, typographers, textile designers, ceramicists, theatrical designers, and craftsmen of all disciplines. This they termed "*Gesamtkunstwerk*" (total artwork) and was an attempt to embrace all areas of life within the total work of art.

GUSTAV KLIMT 1862–1918

Personally quiet and introverted, Klimt was very close to his family and in many ways was a family man without ever actually marrying. He is recorded as having fathered around fourteen children from many different mothers but is only known to have assumed legal responsibility for one, Helene, his brother Ernst's daughter.

Before embarking on a project Klimt would make dozens of sketches and studies and from these it is easy to discern what a sensitive and accomplished artist he was. He is thought to have slept with most, if not all, of the women he painted but— apart from his long-time companion Emilie Flöge—he only seems to have painted one woman twice, the socialite Adele Bloch-Bauer. From unfinished works found in his studio after his death it became apparent that Klimt liked to draw his women naked and then add the layers of clothes and decoration to subsume, muddle, and embellish the images. In his later period he took to creating subtle but richly patterned landscapes, a category of his work that is often overlooked and overshadowed by his more highly charged exotic pictures.

None of this glittering career was likely when Gustav Klimt was born on July 14, 1862, into an impoverished family on the outskirts of Vienna at 247 Linzerstrasse in the Baumgarten (XIV district). He was the second son of Ernst Klimt, a struggling immigrant gold engraver and carver from northern Bohemia, and his wife Anna (née Finster); they went on to have another five children (three boys—Gustav, Ernst, Georg—and four girls—Klara, Hermine, Johanna, and Anna—in total). The family was constantly on the move in the search for cheaper lodgings but it was a close-knit and loving family and the children were always encouraged by their parents to follow their artistic leanings and abilities. When Gustav was eleven a terrible economic recession hit Austria and many people lost their jobs, including his father.

Gustav's artistic talent became apparent at school and led to the suggestion from a relative to his mother that he would really blossom at the School of Applied Arts in Vienna. The school had been established in 1867 as an annex of the Royal and Imperial Austrian Museum for Art and Industry with the function of training students in the widest possible range of arts and crafts' design skills. The intention was to design furniture and other objects which could be made using mass-production techniques to satisfy the artistic desires of the rising middle-class market that aspired to emulate the aristocracy. The school became so successful that by the turn of the twentieth century Vienna was the leading European center for a wide range of cultural activities including sculpture, architecture, literature, and music.

Klimt won a scholarship to the School of Applied Arts and started in 1876 at the age of fourteen. He stayed for seven years until 1883. He was joined in 1877 by his brother Ernst, and the year after that by brother Georg. Gustav and Ernst together with their friend Franz Matsch learned a classical academic range of artistic techniques—especially draftsmanship in the historical style, architectural painting, and crafts like mosaic and fresco—the former as practiced by the hyper-realist artist, Hans Makart, Klimt's greatest early influence. Gustav proved so able that he was quickly moved up to the advanced specialized painting class.

Within three years of commencing study Gustav, Ernst, and Franz became so accomplished that their teachers allowed them to work on their own commercial projects. They named themselves the Künstlercompagnie (Company of Artists) in 1883 (the year Gustav left the School) and worked from a studio at Sandwirtgasse 8 in the VI district. Makart used them to help him in the design and staging of the Grand Festive Procession to celebrate the silver wedding anniversary of Emperor Franz Josef and Elizabeth. In 1880 the three students were commissioned to paint a ceiling for the Sturany Palace, additionally they helped Makart paint murals in the Kunsthistorisches Museum in Vienna.

Painting historic and academic murals and ceilings in the museums, theatres, and churches along the Ringstrasse (such as the Burgtheater staircase decorations, started in 1886) made them wealthy men and helped to lift the Klimt family out of poverty. In addition, Gustav painted portraits of the leading Viennese patrons of the arts.

Although steeped in popular generic paintings, Klimt first started to experiment with the use of gold leaf to add emphasis to his work in 1885 in a small sketch. Three years later, in 1888, while still painting walls and ceilings for the important buildings of Vienna, Emperor Franz Josef I of Austria awarded Klimt the Golden Order of Merit for his work on the murals of the Burgtheater. In addition the Universities of Vienna and Munich awarded him honorary membership. He had become a respectable member of Viennese society. In 1889 he returned to work at the Burgtheater painting portraits of the luminaries of Viennese society and was awarded the Kaiserpreis (Imperial Award) in 1890 for his work there.

In 1891 his brother Ernst Klimt married Helene Flöge and Gustav made one of his first portraits of the bride's younger sister, Emilie Flöge. She was to become the most significant woman in his life, his soul companion, if not his sexual one: their exact relationship is not known but they did stay together until Klimt's death. At much the same time the Künstlercompagnie moved to better studios in the VIII district at Josefstädter Strasse 21.

1892 was a significant year for Klimt: he lost his father and then his brother Ernst (of pericarditis) leaving him to provide for both families. It also signaled the end of the Künstlercompagnie. Ernst was an extremely talented artist and could have emulated his brother and enjoyed a similarly stellar career had he lived longer. (His other brother Georg, was a sculptor and carver and responsible for making Gustav's beautiful picture frames.) These losses affected Klimt deeply and plunged him into an emotional despair that in turn had a noticeable effect on his painting. He became the guardian of Ernst's baby daughter, Helene, and as a consequence saw much more of her aunt, Emilie Flöge. In 1897 both families enjoyed a summer vacation together in Fieberbrunn in the Tyrol.

In the early 1890s the University of Vienna needed its large amphitheater decorated, and invited artistic submissions. After some time, in 1894, the commission was awarded to Klimt and Franz Matsch based on their drafts for the four principal faculties—theology, philosophy, jurisprudence, and medicine. But as they worked on the specifics of the designs their relationship deteriorated until they disagreed so fundamentally that they severed their partnership altogether. The project was delayed for years: eventually Matsch was given Theology but never completed the work and Klimt was given the other three subjects. However, Klimt soon ran into trouble with the authorities: his style had changed from conventional historic scenes to a much more stylized and "modern" interpretation full of allegory and strange allusions. This was not to university's liking or instructions.

When Klimt presented the "Faculty Paintings" (as they became known) to the university, the establishment and public were outraged. *Philosophy* showed strange drifting forms and nudes which critics labeled simplistic—although when he showed it as a work in progress at the Paris World Fair in 1900 he won the Grand Prix. *Jurisprudence* differed greatly from his accepted draft proposition and was criticized as symbolically wrong anyway, but it was *Medicine* that aroused the greatest hostility because not only was its message ambiguous but it was pornographically ambiguous as well.

The public demanded the cancellation of Klimt's commission but the Artistic Advisory Committee of the Ministry of Culture and Education instead sent the paintings to the Vienna State Gallery of Art where they were kept out of sight and discreetly shown to only a select audience. Klimt was furious, declared the work unfinished anyway, and tried to return all the advances he had been paid so he could retrieve the works. The row continued and Klimt's supporter Ritter von Hartel, Minister of Education, was made the scapegoat and forced to resign. The committee finally accepted Klimt's returned fees and he immediately sold the paintings on to August Lederer, a Jewish factory owner and businessman, and his wife Serena. Without any civic commissions Klimt had to rely on private individuals and organizations to earn his living. The Lederers became Klimt's greatest patrons and collectors of his works—but it was to end in tragedy. The Lederers' art collection was seized by the Nazis during World War II and in 1945 the Faculty Paintings were burned by retreating SS troops; their images only remain as photographs.

Infuriated by the whole affair, Klimt severed all his ties with the state. He never received another state commission or even a state-appointed professorship. The Academy of Fine Arts had wanted to appoint Klimt as a professor but the ministry refused to endorse the appointment. His artistic integrity had been questioned and he refused to be censored or have his artistic liberty controlled in any way.

In 1897 Klimt and around forty fellow Austrian artists, sculptors, and architects founded the *Wiener Sezession* (in English, the Vienna Secession) after they resigned *en masse* from the staid confines of the Association of Austrian Artists (Vienna Künstlerhaus). Klimt was elected the first president and Rudolf von Alt, the architectural painter, became the first honorary president. Klimt's work *Pallas Athene* (1898) was chosen as its symbol.

The intention of the Secession was to showcase the work of young modern Austrian artists and bring the best foreign art, especially the French Impressionists, to Vienna. Their other remit was to publish a regular magazine, *Ver Sacrum* (Sacrifice), explaining and publicizing their work. The first Sezession exhibition was a great success: twenty-three Viennese painters showed their work alongside 131 works from foreigners; some 57,000 visitors walked through the exhibition, including the Kaiser, and over a third of the exhibits were sold.

In 1898, in recognition of his pioneering work, Klimt was made an honorary member of the International

Society of Artists, Sculptors, and Engravers of London. Again that summer the Klimt and the Flöge families holidayed together at St. Agatha in the Salzkammergut, Austria.

Although the Secession was unconventional, the group was supported by the Austrian government, especially after the great success of the first show. The outcome of this was a long-term lease on public land near Karlsplatz where the Secession erected its iconic exhibition hall in 1898. The building was designed by Joseph Maria Olbrich after drawings by Klimt and was completed in six months. Above the main door the inscription reads, "Give our time its art, and art its freedom." The Secession Hall immediately became the leading international exhibition center and the Secession the most important artists' association in Vienna making the city as important an artistic center as London or Paris.

In 1899 Klimt painted *Schubert at the Piano* for the music room at the Palais Dumba. The main model for the work was Maria Zimmermann who became the mother of Gustav and Otto Zimmermann, two of Klimt's illegitimate children. Sadly the infant Otto was to die in 1903 leaving Klimt obsessed with death themes.

The summer of 1900 saw the Klimt and Flöge families start the first of their regular summer vacations at the island chateau of Litzlberg on Attersee Lake in the Salzkammergut area of Austria.

Klimt was central to the work and international recognition of the Secession: he was its chief spokesman, a prime selector of exhibition material (the Secession was the first association to exhibit by theme rather than by individual artist), and part of the editorial staff and graphic artist for *Ver Sacrum*.

Possibly because of their initial poverty the Klimt family were very close and important to each other: in fact, Klimt had dealings with them all almost daily throughout his life. Regardless of personal success Gustav was quiet and rather introverted, he was something of a loner and according to one of his sisters needed constant reassurance of their love and total support so he could be free to concentrate on his work. His sister Hermine Klimt wrote, "... Once he had gathered strength, he would plunge into his work with such vehemence that we often thought the flames of his genius might consume him alive."

In 1902 the Secession held its XIV Beethoven Exhibition, celebrating the musician's "vision of universal brotherhood where the whole of Mankind would be set free of its pains." On the first night Gustav Mahler directed the Fourth part of Beethoven's Ninth Symphony, and over its duration the exhibition attracted 58,000 visitors. Klimt contributed his seventy-foot long *Beethoven Frieze*. Intended to be a temporary decoration, the work was painted on inexpensive material in three main sections and follows the journey of a medieval knight on his quest for human salvation. The first panel is *Desire for Happiness* and shows the knight deciding to take up the struggle. Panel two, *Encounters During Struggle*, depicts the knight overcoming hostile forces with the use of weapons such as poetry. Panel three, *Salvation*, shows him finding love.

In 1903 the XVIII exhibition was devoted entirely to eighty of Klimt's pictures. That same year designers Josef Hoffmann, Koloman Moser, and the financier Fritz Wärndorfer founded the *Wiener Werkstätte* (Vienna Workshop) community of visual artists dedicated to creating affordable art for everyone. Klimt joined the workshop but also found the time to travel to Italy where he visited Ravenna, Venice, Padua, Florence, and Pisa. There he found inspiration from the richness of the Renaissance art to start working with elaborate ornamentation and gold.

Inevitably, as with any group of artists and egos, there were arguments and ruptures in the Secession. Eventually Klimt—along with Hoffmann, Moser, Otto Wagner, and Carl Moll as well as others, collectively labeled the *Klimt-Gruppe*—left and set up the rival Austrian National Union of Artists (aka Art Show, 1905) with the intention of making affordable, well-designed products accessible for everyone, not just the wealthy. With Klimt's departure the Secession rapidly lost credibility and influence. By this time anyway Jugendstil and Art Nouveau had become "establishment" as high society accepted modernism and there was little left for contemporary artists' to rail against.

From this period onward Klimt predominantly painted portraits and landscapes, although he also started to sketch out his ideas for the mosaic frieze at the Stoclet Palace. It is worth pointing out, however, that by this time he was increasingly regarded as old-fashioned by his younger contemporaries such as Oskar Kokoschka and Egon Schiele, who aimed to stretch the reach of modernism.

1906 saw the start of Klimt's "Golden Period" (1906–09) with the portrait of Fritza Riedler and her elaborate gold-textured dress. He had experimented with gold leaf throughout his career, using it for halos and decorative emphasis, but during this period he used great fields of gold to emphasize the preciousness of the image and to add a baroque richness. The following year he painted an even golder and more elaborate portrait of the noted society hostess Adele Bloch-Bauer.

For the 1908 First Vienna Kunstschau (Art Show) exhibition Klimt showed sixteen paintings in a hall devoted to his work. The centerpiece of the show was *The Kiss* (1907–08), a riot of gold, pattern and sinuous line— although at this period the painting was unfinished. Unlike many of his previous sensual paintings, the critics and public loved it, so much so that the Austrian State Gallery bought it.

The hugely wealthy Belgian civil railroad engineer and financier, Adolphe Stoclet, wanted an opulent villa (initially in Vienna and then changed to Brussels) and gave the architect Josef Hoffmann an unlimited budget to design and construct a stunning avant-garde building. In turn Hoffmann commissioned Gustav Klimt and Fernand Khnopff to do much of the interior decoration. The resulting Stoclet Palace—at 279–81 avenue de Tervuren, Brussels—became a modernist masterpiece.

Between 1909 and 1911 Klimt worked at the Stoclet Palace; by then over his Golden Period he used gold leaf with more restraint before abandoning it almost altogether. Klimt was given the dining room to decorate. He devised an opulent frieze to run around the room entitled *The New Cycle of Life* which incorporates a stylized three-part mosaic: *Expectation* (showing a woman dancing and searching), *Fulfillment* (showing an embracing man and woman enveloped in a patterned cloak), and *Pattern* (an ambiguous riot of pattern which shows a person who might be God, and possible new life being created). The mosaic was constructed in the Wiener Werkstätte workshop in Vienna and used the gamut of precious and semi-precious stones plus gold leaf and silver. These were the last wall decorations Klimt made.

Klimt was by then working in what has been termed his Later Period and noticeably using much less gold. Instead, his palette was much brighter after being influenced by Matisse whose work was exhibited at the 1909 Art Show. Other changes include replacing pattern with flowers and an altogether simpler, less elaborate approach to decoration.

He started *Salome* (*Judith II*) in 1907 and finished in 1910 when it was shown at the Venice Biennale. It became the sensation of the show and was bought by the city of Venice: it now hangs at the Palazzo di Ca'Pesaro. By this time Klimt's paintings were shown regularly in important art exhibitions around Europe.

Gustav Klimt moved to his last studio in 1912, a one-story garden-surrounded Biedermeier-style house at Feldmühlgasse in the XIII district. He also became president of the Bund Oesterreichischer Künstler artistic association, and he started the first of his annual taking of the waters at Bad Gastein with Emilie Flöge at his side.

In 1915 Klimt was shattered by the death of his mother at the age of 79 (she and one of his sisters suffered from mental illness) and his palette noticeably darkens. Four years earlier he had painted *Death and Life* and

given it a shimmering golden river through the center—it was awarded first prize at the International Art Exhibition in Rome—but with the loss of his beloved mother he painted over the gold with a greyish-black wash.

The last years of his life saw Klimt painting and exhibiting regularly and still receiving accolades: the 1916 World's Fair in Berlin showcased his work alongside that of Oskar Kokoschka, Egon Schiele, and Anton Faistauer, and the following year he was elected honorary member of the academies of fine art in Vienna and Munich.

On January 11, 1918, Klimt suffered a stroke while at home in Westbahnstrasse 36 in the VII district, from which he never recovered. He died a few weeks later of pneumonia in the General Hospital in Vienna on February 6, at the age of 55. He left a large estate; fifteen people came forward claiming to be his children, probably hoping to inherit a healthy reward. He was honored with a plot at the Hietzing Cemetery and given a funeral there three days later by the Austrian state. The newspapers were full of eulogies and obituaries.

As a tragic footnote to Klimt's career, the explanation for the paucity of his great works on show today stems from events already mentioned at the end of World War II. The Nazis were notorious for looting art and Klimt's works were especially prized. The collection of August and Serena Lederer was taken from Vienna "to protect them" from harm and hung in Schloss Immendorf in southern Austria. In 1945, as SS troops were retreating back to Germany, they stayed the night at the schloss, apparently drinking and raising mayhem. When they left in the morning they blew the castle up rather than leave the Klimts and other treasures for the Soviets to loot. Thirteen Klimts were destroyed in the subsequent fire including *Schubert at the Piano* (1899), *Procession of the Dead* (1903), *Medicine* with its detail of the stunning Hygeia, *Philosophy*, and *Jurisprudence* (1899–1907) and one of his last works, the landscape *Gastein* (1917).

Plate 1

FABLE
1883; 33.25 x 46 inch (84.5 x 117 cm); Oil on canvas.
Historical Museum, Vienna

Plate 2

IDYLL

1884; 19.5 x 30 inch (49.5 x 73.5 cm); Oil on canvas
Historical Museum, Vienna

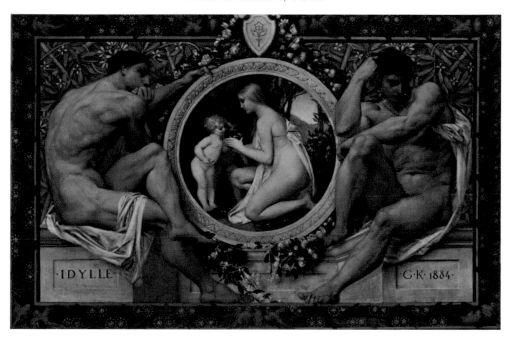

Plate 3

THE THEATER OF TAORMINA

1886–1888; 295.2 × 157.4 inch (750 × 400 cm); Oil on canvas.
Burgtheater, Vienna

Plate 4

THE OLD BURGTHEATER
1888; 32.3 x 36.2 inch (82 x 92 cm); Oil on canvas.
Wien Museum, Vienna

Plate 5

SAPPHO
1888-1890; 15.35 × 12.44 inch (39 × 31.6 cm); Oil on canvas
Historical Museum, Vienna

Plate 6

FLOWING WATER
1889; 20.5 x 25.6 inch (52 x 65 cm); Oil on canvas
Private Collection

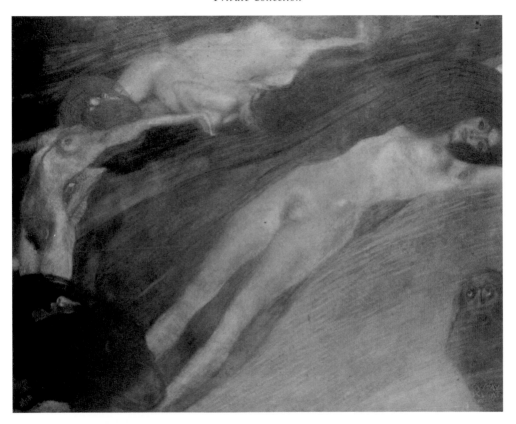

Plate 7

JOSEPH PEMBAUER

1890; 21.7 x 27.2 inch (55 x 69 cm); Oil on canvas.
Tyrolean State Museum Ferdinandeum, Innsbruck

Plate 8

PORTRAIT OF A LADY (FRAU HEYMANN)

1894; 9.1 x 15.4 inch (23 x 39 cm); Oil on canvas.
Historical Museum, Vienna

Plate 9

LOVE
1895; 17.3 x 23.6 inch (44 x 60 cm); Oil on canvas.
Historical Museum, Vienna

Plate 10

MUSIC I

1895; 14.6 x 17.7 inch (37 x 45 cm); Oil on canvas.
Alte Pinakothek, Munich, Bavaria, Germany

Plate 11

ACTOR JOSEF LEWINSKY AS CARLOS
1895; 17.3 x 25.2 inch (44 x 64 cm); Oil on canvas.
Osterreichische Galerie, Vienna, Austria

Plate 12

PORTRAIT OF HELENE KLIMT

1898; 23.6 x 15.7 inch (60 x 40 cm); Oil on canvas
Osterreichische Galerie, Vienna, Austria

Plate 13

PALLAS ATHENE

1898; 29.5 x 29.5 inch (75 x 75 cm); Oil on canvas.
Osterreichische Galerie, Vienna, Austria

Plate 14

PORTRAIT OF SONJA KNIPS
1898; 57.1 x 57.1 inch (145 x 145 cm); Oil on canvas.
Osterreichische Galerie, Vienna, Austria

Plate 15

PORTRAIT OF A WOMAN

1898/99; 17.7 x 13.3 inch (45 × 34 cm); Oil on canvas.
Österreichische Galerie, Wien, Austria

Plate 16

PORTRAIT OF SERENA LEDERER
1899; 33.6 x 74.0 inch (85.4 x 188 cm); Oil on canvas.
The Museum of Modern Art, New York, NY

Plate 17

NUDA VERITAS
1899; 102.3 x 25.4 inch (260 x 64.5 cm); Oil on canvas
Austrian National Library, Vienna, Austria

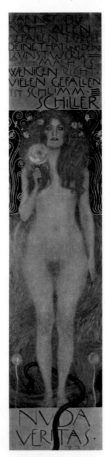

Plate 18

AFTER THE RAIN
1899; 15.7 x 31.5 inch (40 x 80 cm); Oil on canvas.
Vienna, Osterreichische Museum für Angewandte Kunst

Plate 19

MERMAIDS (WHITEFISH)
1899; 20.5 x 32.3 inch (52 x 82 cm); Oil on canvas.
Zentralsparkasse, Vienna

Plate 20

QUIET POND IN THE PARK OF APPEAL
1899; 29.13 × 29.13 inch (74 × 74 cm); Oil on canvas.
Sammlung Leopold, Vienna, Austria

Plate 21

SCHUBERT AT THE PIANO
1899; 59.1 x 78.7 inch (150 x 200 cm); Oil on canvas.
Destroyed by fire at Immendorf Palace, 1945

Plate 22

FARMHOUSE WITH BIRCH TREES
1900; 31.5 x 31.5 inch (80 x 80 cm); Oil on canvas
Osterreichische Galerie, Vienna, Austria

Plate 23

JUDITH I
1901; 33 x 16.5 inch (84 × 42 cm); Oil on canvas
Osterreichische Galerie, Vienna, Austria

Plate 24

COWS IN THE BARN

1901; 29.5 x 29.5 inch (75 × 75 cm); Oil on canvas
Neue Galerie der Stadt, Wolfgang-Gurlitt-Museum, Linz

Plate 25

BEETHOVEN FRIEZE (DETAIL)
1902; 86.6 x 250.4 inch (220 x 636 cm); Oil on canvas.
Osterreichische Galerie, Vienna, Austria

Plate 26

THE BEETHOVEN FRIEZE
1902
Osterreichische Galerie, Vienna, Austria

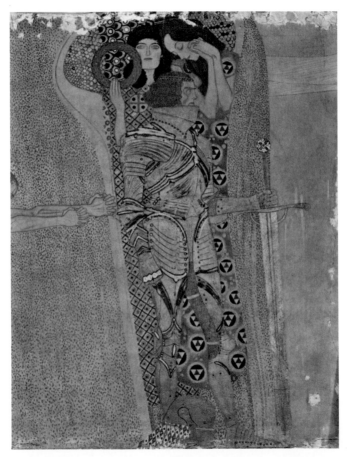

Plate 27

BEECH FOREST I
1902; 39.4 x 39.4 inch (100 x 100 cm); Oil on canvas.
Staatliche Kunstsammlungen Dresden, Germany

Plate 28

GOLD FISH
1902; 18.1 x 59.1 inch (46 x 150 cm); Oil on canvas
Kunstmuseum, Winterthur, Switzerland

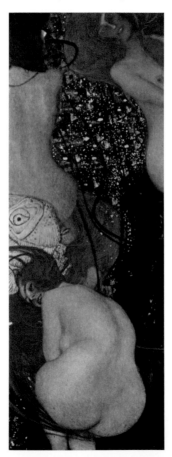

Plate 29

PORTRAIT OF EMILIE FLOGE

1902; 26.2 x 71.3 inch (66.5 x 181 cm); Oil on canvas.
Historisches Museum der Stadt Wien, Vienna

Plate 30

BIRCH WOOD

1903; 43.3 x 43.3 inch (110 x 110 cm); Oil on canvas.
Osterreichische Galerie, Vienna, Austria

Plate 31

THE GREAT POPLAR
1903; 39.3 x 39.3 inch (100 x 100 cm); Oil on canvas.
Leopold-Museum, Vienna

Plate 32

PORTRAIT OF HERMINE GALLIA

1904; 37.8 x 66.9 inch (96 x 170 cm); Oil on canvas.
The National Gallery, London, England

Plate 33

HOPE I

1903; 26.4 x 74.4 inch (67 x 189 cm); Oil on canvas.
National Gallery of Canada, Ottawa

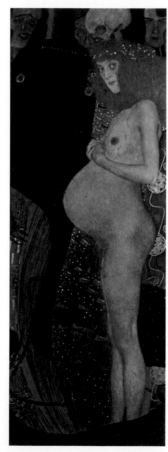

Plate 34

THE STOCLET FRIEZE
1905-09; 77.5 × 35.8 inch (197 × 91 cm); Oil on canvas
Osterreichische Galerie, Vienna, Austria

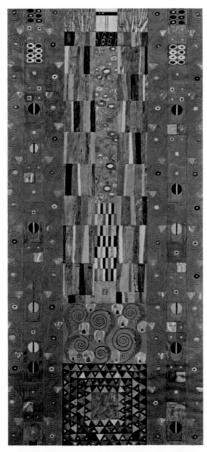

Plate 35

STOCLET FRIEZE: EXPECTATION
1905; 193 x 115 cm; Mixed on paper
Österreichische Galerie, Vienna, Austria

STOCLET FRIEZE: FULFILMENT

Plate 36

1905; 194 x 121 cm; Mixed on paper
Osterreichische Galerie, Vienna, Austria

Plate 37

STOCLET FRIEZE: TREE OF LIFE
1905; 40.2 x 76.8 inch (102 x 195 cm); Oil on canvas.
Osterreichische Galerie, Vienna, Austria

Plate 38

THE THREE AGES OF WOMAN
1905; 70.1 x 78.0 inch (178 x 198 cm); Oil on canvas.
Galleria Nazionale d'Arte Moderna, Rome, Italy

Plate 39

FARM GARDEN WITH SUNFLOWERS
1905; 43.3 x 43.3 inch (110 x 110 cm); Oil on canvas
Osterreichische Galerie, Vienna, Austria

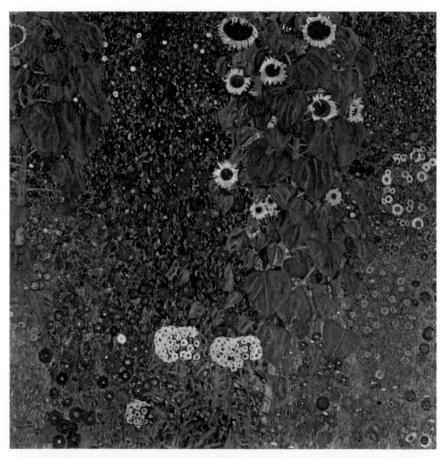

Plate 40

PORTRAIT OF MARGARET STONBOROUGH-WITTGENSTEIN

1905; 35.4 x 70.9 inch (90 x 180 cm); Oil on canvas.
Alte Pinakothek, Munich, Bavaria, Germany

Plate 41

PORTRAIT OF FRIEDERIKE MARIA BEER
1906; 66.14 × 51.18 inch (168 × 130 cm); Oil on canvas.
Tel Aviv Museum of Art

Plate 42

PORTRAIT OF FRITZA RIEDLER
1906; 52.4 x 60.2 inch (133 x 153 cm); Oil on canvas.
Osterreichische Galerie, Vienna, Austria

Plate 43

THE KISS
1907; 70.9 x 70.9 inch (180 x 180 cm); Oil on canvas.
Osterreichische Galerie, Vienna, Austria

Plate 44

DANAE

1907; 30.3 x 32.7 inch (77 x 83 cm); Oil on canvas.
Rome, Galleria Nazionale d'Arte Moderna

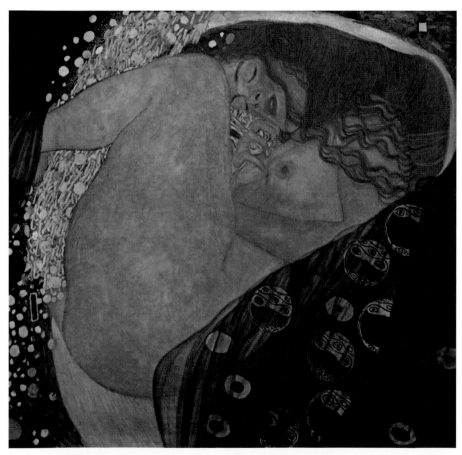

Plate 45

POPPY FIELD

1907; 43.3 x 43.3 inch (110 x 110 cm); Oil on canvas
Osterreichische Galerie, Vienna, Austria

Plate 46

PORTRAIT OF ADELE BLOCH-BAUER I
1907; 54.3 x 54.3 inch (138 x 138 cm); Oil on canvas.
Osterreichische Galerie, Vienna, Austria

Plate 47

WATER SERPENTS I

1907; 7.9 x 19.7 inch (20 x 50 cm); Oil on canvas.
Osterreichische Galerie, Vienna, Austria

Plate 48

WATER SERPENTS II

1907; 31.5 x 57.1 inch (80 x 145 cm); Oil on canvas.
Rome, Galleria Nazionale d'Arte Moderna

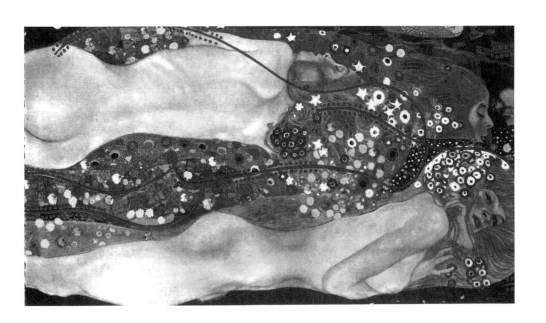

Plate 49

HOPE II

1907; 43.3 x 43.3 inch (110 x 110 cm); Oil on canvas.
The Museum of Modern Art, New York, NY

Plate 50

FLOWERING FIELD

1909; 39.4 x 39.4 inch (100 x 100 cm); Oil on canvas.
Carnegie Museum of Art, Pittsburgh, PA

Plate 51

LADY WITH HAT AND FEATHER BOA

1909; 21.7 x 27.2 inch (55 x 69 cm); Oil on canvas.
Osterreichische Galerie, Vienna, Austria

THE PARK

Plate 52

1910; 43.3 x 43.3 inch (110 x 110 cm); Oil on canvas.
The Museum of Modern Art, New York, NY

Plate 53

THE BLACK FEATHER HAT
1910; 31.1 x 24.8 inch (79 x 63 cm); Oil on canvas.
Rome, Galleria Nazionale d'Arte Moderna

Plate 54

SCHLOB KAMMER ON THE ATTERSEE III
1910; 43.3 x 43.3 inch (110 x 110 cm); Oil on canvas.
Osterreichische Galerie, Vienna, Austria

Plate 55

FARMHOUSE IN UPPER AUSTRIA
1911/12; 43.3 x 43.3 inch (110 x 110 cm); Oil on canvas
Osterreichische Galerie, Vienna, Austria

Plate 56

DAS HAUS VON GUARDABOSCHI
1912; 43.31 × 43.31 inch (110 × 110 cm); Oil on canvas.
Neue Galerie, New York, NY

Plate 57

PORTRAIT OF ADELE BLOCH-BAUER II
1912; 47.2 x 74.8 inch (120 x 190 cm); Oil on canvas.
Osterreichische Galerie, Vienna, Austria

Plate 58

PORTRAIT OF MADA PRIMAVESI
1912; 43.5 x 59.1 inch (110.5 x 150 cm); Oil on canvas.
The Metropolitan Museum of Art, New York, NY

Plate 59

AVENUE IN SCHLOSS KAMMER PARK

1912; 43.3 x 43.3 inch (110 x 110 cm); Oil on canvas.
Vienna, Osterreichische Museum für Angewandte Kunst

Plate 60

MALCESINE ON LAKE GARDA
1913; 43.3 x 43.3 inch (110 x 110 cm); Oil on canvas.
Burned in Schlob Immendorf, Austria, 1945

Plate 61

THE VIRGIN

1913; 74.8 x 78.7 inch (190 x 200 cm); Oil on canvas.
National Gallery, Prague, Czech Republic

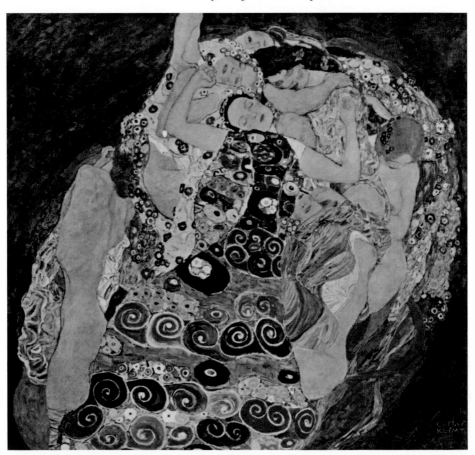

Plate 62

CHURCH IN CASSONE

1913; 43.3 x 43.3 inch (110 x 110 cm); Oil on canvas.
Rome, Galleria Nazionale d'Arte Moderna

Plate 63

PORTRAIT OF BARONESS ELISABETH BACCHOFEN-ECHT
c. 1914; 70.8 x 49.6 inch (180 × 126 cm); Oil on canvas.
Private Collection

Plate 64

PORTRAIT OF EUGENIA PRIMAVESI
1914; 33.1 x 55.1 inch (84 x 140 cm); Oil on canvas.
Private collection

Plate 65

UNTERACH ON LAKE ATTERSEE
1915; 43.3 x 43.3 inch (110 x 110 cm); Oil on canvas.
Rupertinum, Salzburg State Collections

Plate 66

GIRL FRIENDS (DETAIL)
1916; Oil on canvas.
Destroyed by fire in 1945

Plate 67

APPLE TREE II
1916; 31.5 x 31.5 inch (80 x 80 cm); Oil on canvas.
Osterreichische Galerie, Vienna, Austria

Plate 68

CHURCH IN UNTERACH ON THE ATTERSEE
1916; 43.3 x 43.3 inch (110 x 110 cm); Oil on canvas.
Rome, Galleria Nazionale d'Arte Moderna

Plate 69

GARDEN PATH WITH CHICKENS

1916; 43.3 x 43.3 inch (110 x 110 cm); Oil on canvas
Burned in Schlob Immendorf, Austria, 1945

Plate 70

DEATH AND LIFE
1916; 70.1 x 78.0 inch (178 x 198 cm); Oil on canvas.
Private Collection

Plate 71

PORTRAIT OF A LADY

1916/17; 23.6 x 21.6 inch (60 × 55 cm); Oil on canvas.
Galleria Ricci-Oddi, Piacenza, Italy

Plate 72

LADY WITH A FAN
1917/18; 39.3 x 39.3 inch (100 x 100 cm); Oil on canvas.
Leopold-Museum, Vienna

91

Plate 73

ADAM AND EVE
1917 - 18; 173 x 60 cm; Oil on canvas.
Vienna, Österreichische Museum für Angewandte Kunst

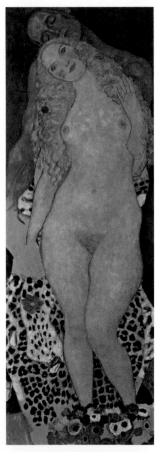

Plate 74

BABY (DETAIL)

1918; 43.3 x 43.3 inch (110 x 110 cm); Oil on canvas.
Washington, National Gallery of Art

Plate 75

PORTRAIT OF JOHANNA STAUDE

1918; 19.7 x 27.6 inch (50 x 70 cm); Oil on canvas.
Historical Museum, Vienna

Plate 76

PORTRAIT OF A LADY

1918; 35.4 x 70.9 inch (90 x 180 cm); Oil on canvas.
Wolfgang-Gurlitt-Museum, Linz